CHRISTMAS FAVORITES

Solos and String Orchestra Arrangements
Correlated with Essential Elements String Metho[d]

Arranged by
LLOYD CONLEY

Welcome to Essential Elements Christmas Favorites! There are two versions of each selection in this versatile book. The SOLO version appears in the beginning of your book. The STRING ORCHESTRA arrangements of each song follows. The supplemental recording (CD or Cassette) or string orchestra PIANO PART may be used as an accompaniment for solo performance. Use these recordings when playing solos for friends and family.

ISBN 978-0-7935-8394-2

HAL•LEONARD®
CORPORATION
7777 W. BLUEMOUND RD. P.O. BOX 13819 MILWAUKEE, WI 53213

Copyright © 1997 by HAL LEONARD CORPORATION
International Copyright Secured   All Rights Reserved

JINGLE BELLS

STRING BASS
Solo

Words and Music by J. PIERPONT
Arranged by LLOYD CONLEY

00868014

Copyright © 1997 by HAL LEONARD CORPORATION
International Copyright Secured   All Rights Reserved

UP ON THE HOUSETOP

STRING BASS
Solo

Words and Music by B.R. HANDY
Arranged by LLOYD CONLEY

Moderately Fast

5 Up on the house - top—— rein - deer pause, Out jumps

good old San - ta Claus; **13** Down through the

chim - ney with lots of toys, All for the lit - tle ones,

Christ - mas joys. **21** Ho, ho, ho! Who would - n't

go! Ho, ho, ho! Who would - n't

go! **29** Up on the house - top, click, click,

click, Down through the chim - ney with good

Saint Nick.

Copyright © 1997 by HAL LEONARD CORPORATION
International Copyright Secured   All Rights Reserved

THE HANUKKAH SONG

STRING BASS
Solo

Traditional
Arranged by LLOYD CONLEY

00868014

Copyright © 1997 by HAL LEONARD CORPORATION
International Copyright Secured   All Rights Reserved

STRING BASS
Solo

Traditional English Folksong
Arranged by LLOYD CONLEY

Copyright © 1997 by HAL LEONARD CORPORATION
International Copyright Secured   All Rights Reserved

STRING BASS
Solo

Music and Lyrics by JOHNNY MARKS
Arranged by LLOYD CONLEY

00868014
Copyright © 1962, 1964 (Renewed 1990, 1992) St. Nicholas Music Inc., 1619 Broadway, New York, New York 10019
This arrangement Copyright © 1997 St. Nicholas Music Inc.
All Rights Reserved

FROSTY THE SNOWMAN

STRING BASS
Solo

Words and Music by
STEVE NELSON and **JACK ROLLINS**
Arranged by LLOYD CONLEY

Copyright © 1950 by Chappell & Co.
Copyright Renewed
This arrangement Copyright © 1997 by Chappell & Co.
International Copyright Secured   All Rights Reserved

00868014

--KIN' A--UN-- T-E C-- --TMA- T -EE

STRING BASS
Solo

Music and Lyrics by JOHNNY MARKS
Arranged by LLOYD CONLEY

00868014

Copyright © 1958 (Renewed 1986) St. Nicholas Music Inc., 1619 Broadway, New York, New York 10019
This arrangement Copyright © 1997 St. Nicholas Music Inc.
All Rights Reserved

JINGLE-BELL ROCK

STRING BASS
Solo

Words and Music by
JOE BEAL and JIM BOOTHE
Arranged by **LLOYD CONLEY**

Jin - gle-bell, Jin - gle-bell, Jin - gle-bell rock   jin - gle-bell swing and
Jin - gle-bell, Jin - gle-bell, Jin - gle-bell rock   jin - gle-bell chime in

jin - gle-bells ring. Snow - in' and blow - in' up bush - els of fun   Now the jin - gle-hop
jin - gle-bell time. Danc - in' and pranc - in' in Jin - gle-bell Square

has be - gun.   in the fros - ty air. What a

right   time   to   rock

swell   time   to   go glid - in' in a one - horse sleigh. Gid - dy - ap

pick   up   your   feet.

jin - gle - in' beat. That's the jin - gle-bell rock. What a

long.   Gid - dy - ap, jin - gle-horse pick up your feet

clock.   Mix   and   min - gle in a jin - gle - in' beat.____

That's the jin - gle - bell,   That's the   jin - gle - bell   rock.

Copyright © 1957 by Chappell & Co.
Copyright Renewed
This arrangement Copyright © 1997 by Chappell & Co.
International Copyright Secured   All Rights Reserved

00868014

silver bells

From the Paramount Picture THE LEMON DROP KID

STRING BASS
Solo

Words and Music by
JAY LIVINGSTON and RAY EVANS
Arranged by LLOYD CONLEY

Christ - mas makes you feel e - mo - tion - al.
It may bring par - ties or thoughts de - vo - tion - al. What - ev - er
hap - pens or what may be, Here is what Christ - mas time
means to me.___ Cit - y side - walks, bus - y side - walks dressed in hol - i - day
style. In the air there's a feel - ing of Christ - mas.___ Chil - dren
smile, And on ev - 'ry street cor - ner you hear. Sil - ver bells,___
Sil - ver bells,___ It's Christ - mas time in the cit - y.___
Ring - a - ling,___ hear them ring,___
Soon it will be Christ - mas day.

Copyright © 1950 (Renewed 1977) by Paramount Music Corporation
This arrangement Copyright © 1997 by Paramount Music Corporation
International Copyright Secured   All Rights Reserved

LET IT SNOW! LET IT SNOW! LET IT SNOW!

STRING BASS
Solo

Words by SAMMY CAHN
Music by JULE STYNE
Arranged by LLOYD CONLEY

Copyright © 1945 by Producers Music Publishing Co. and Cahn Music Co.
Copyright Renewed
This arrangement Copyright © 1997 by Producers Music Publishing Co. and Cahn Music Co.
All Rights on behalf of Producers Music Publishing Co. Administered by Chappell & Co.
All Rights on behalf of Cahn Music Co. Administered by WB Music Corp.
International Copyright Secured   All Rights Reserved

00868014

WHITE CHRISTMAS

From the Motion Picture Irving Berlin's HOLIDAY INN

STRING BASS
Solo

Words and Music by IRVING BERLIN
Arranged by LLOYD CONLEY

I'm dream-ing of a white Christ-mas, Just like the ones I used to know. Where the tree-tops glis-ten and chil-dren lis-ten to hear sleigh-bells in the snow. I'm dream-ing of a white Christ-mas, With ev-'ry Christ-mas card I write, "May your days be mer-ry and bright, And may all your Christ-mas-es be white."

© Copyright 1940, 1942 by Irving Berlin
Copyright Renewed
This arrangement © Copyright 1997 by the Estate of Irving Berlin
International Copyright Secured   All Rights Reserved

00868014

JINGLE BELLS

STRING BASS
String Orchestra Arrangement

Words and Music by J. PIERPONT
Arranged by LLOYD CONLEY

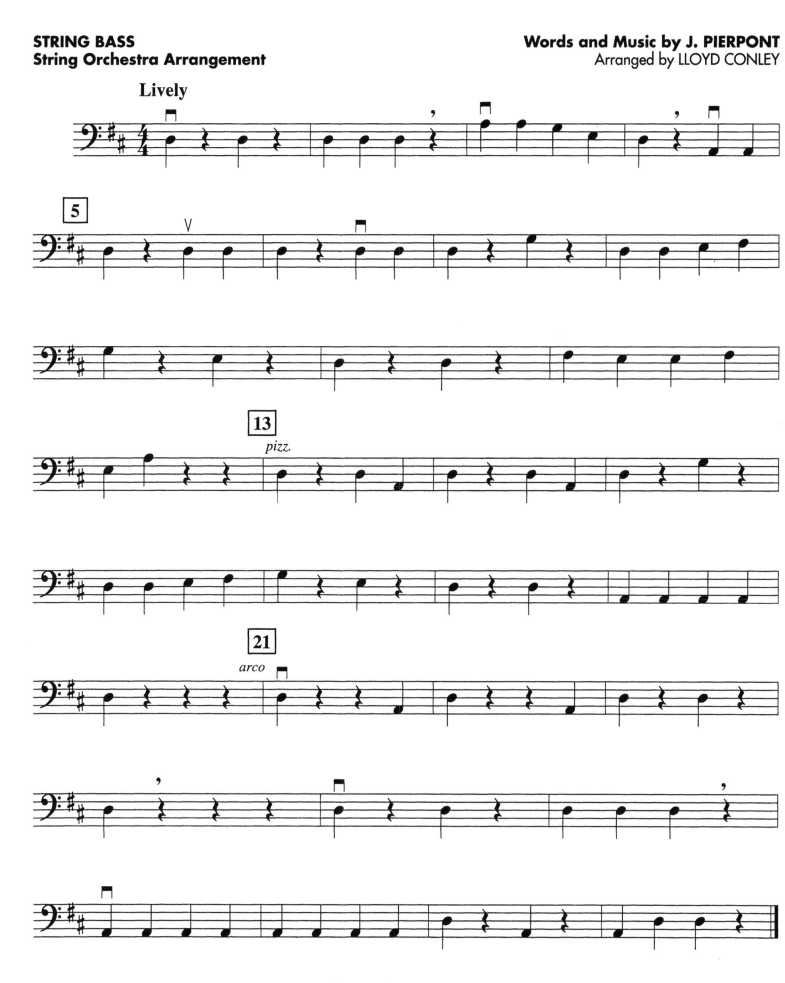

Copyright © 1997 by HAL LEONARD CORPORATION
International Copyright Secured   All Rights Reserved

STRING BASS
String Orchestra Arrangement

Words and Music by B.R. HANDY
Arranged by LLOYD CONLEY

Copyright © 1997 by HAL LEONARD CORPORATION
International Copyright Secured   All Rights Reserved

00868014

STRING BASS
String Orchestra Arrangement

Traditional
Arranged by LLOYD CONLEY

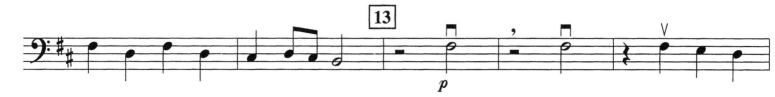

Copyright © 1997 by HAL LEONARD CORPORATION
International Copyright Secured   All Rights Reserved

WE WISH YOU A MERRY CHRISTMAS

STRING BASS
String Orchestra Arrangement

Traditional English Folksong
Arranged by LLOYD CONLEY

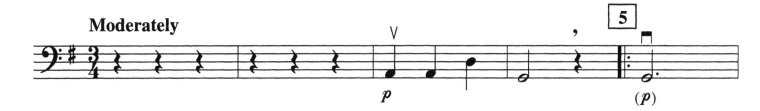

Copyright © 1997 by HAL LEONARD CORPORATION
International Copyright Secured   All Rights Reserved

00868014

STRING BASS
String Orchestra Arrangement

Music and Lyrics by JOHNNY MARKS
Arranged by LLOYD CONLEY

Copyright © 1962, 1964 (Renewed 1990, 1992) St. Nicholas Music Inc., 1619 Broadway, New York, New York 10019
This arrangement Copyright © 1997 St. Nicholas Music Inc.
All Rights Reserved

FROSTY THE SNOWMAN

**Words and Music by
STEVE NELSON and JACK ROLLINS**
Arranged by LLOYD CONLEY

STRING BASS
String Orchestra Arrangement

Copyright © 1950 by Chappell & Co.
Copyright Renewed
This arrangement Copyright © 1997 by Chappell & Co.
International Copyright Secured   All Rights Reserved

00868014

STRING BASS
String Orchestra Arrangement

Music and Lyrics by JOHNNY MARKS
Arranged by LLOYD CONLEY

Copyright © 1958 (Renewed 1986) St. Nicholas Music Inc., 1619 Broadway, New York, New York 10019
This arrangement Copyright © 1997 St. Nicholas Music Inc.
All Rights Reserved

00868014

JINGLE BELL ROCK

Words and Music by
JOE BEAL and **JIM BOOTHE**
Arranged by LLOYD CONLEY

STRING BASS
String Orchestra Arrangement

Copyright © 1957 by Chappell & Co.
Copyright Renewed
This arrangement Copyright © 1997 by Chappell & Co.
International Copyright Secured   All Rights Reserved

00868014

SILVER BELLS
From the Paramount Picture THE LEMON DROP KID

STRING BASS
String Orchestra Arrangement

Words and Music by
JAY LIVINGSTON and RAY EVANS
Arranged by LLOYD CONLEY

Copyright © 1950 (Renewed 1977) by Paramount Music Corporation
This arrangement Copyright © 1997 by Paramount Music Corporation
International Copyright Secured   All Rights Reserved

00868014

LET IT SNOW! LET IT SNOW! LET IT SNOW!

STRING BASS
String Orchestra Arrangement

Words by SAMMY CAHN
Music by JULE STYNE
Arranged by LLOYD CONLEY

Copyright © 1945 by Producers Music Publishing Co. and Cahn Music Co.
Copyright Renewed
This arrangement Copyright © 1997 by Producers Music Publishing Co. and Cahn Music Co.
All Rights on behalf of Producers Music Publishing Co. Administered by Chappell & Co.
All Rights on behalf of Cahn Music Co. Administered by WB Music Corp.
International Copyright Secured   All Rights Reserved

0868014

W ITE HRI TM

From the Motion Picture Irving Berlin's HOLIDAY INN

STRING BASS
String Orchestra Arrangement

Words and Music by
IRVING BERLIN
Arranged by LLOYD CONLEY

Moderately

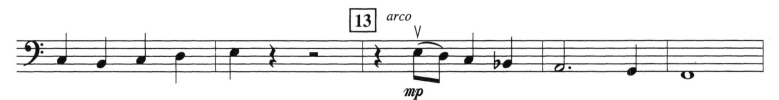

© Copyright 1940, 1942 by Irving Berlin
Copyright Renewed
This arrangement © Copyright 1997 by the Estate of Irving Berlin
International Copyright Secured   All Rights Reserved